THE KEA'S GUIDE TO GETTING WHAT YOU WANT

THE KEA'S GUIDE TO GETTING WHAT YOU WANT

Life advice from the world's smartest bird

Harper *by* Design

KEA ORA!

If you want to get ahead in life, who better to ask than a kea?
Masters of mischief, they boldly go wherever they bloody well like,
staring down – or simply ignoring – anyone who tries to get in their way.

There's a reason a flock of kea is called a circus – or a conspiracy.
With their love of pranks and noisy laugh, they're sometimes called 'the
clowns of the Alps', but don't be deceived. They're smarter than the average
bird, with a sophistication and sly intelligence that might surprise you.

Kea are the original stickybeaks, highly observant and nosy as.
They'll investigate anything you're foolish enough to leave within their
reach: your backpack, your chillybin – even your car, if you leave the
door open. These birds know what they want, and when they see it, they
take it. To achieve more ambitious goals – like stealing your passport
or letting down your tyres – they'll pair up or work in a team.

What's more, they get away with it. The kea is the definitive hard case,
its outrageous antics amusing, even awe-inspiring.

By following the example of this beloved national icon,
you too can succeed. All you need is this guide!

ALWAYS PUT YOUR BEST FOOT FORWARD.

KNOW WHERE YOU
WANT TO GO ...

AND HOW YOU'RE GOING TO GET THERE.

FOCUS ON WHERE YOU'RE HEADED, NOT WHERE YOU'VE BEEN.

KEEP AN
EYE OUT FOR
OPPORTUNITIES.

YOU NEVER KNOW WHAT'S JUST AROUND THE CORNER.

CAUTION

NEXT 5 km

BE READY TO STRIKE WHEN OTHERS LET THEIR GUARD DOWN.

OR FENCE YOU IN.

WATCH HOW EXPERTS DO IT.

DON'T WAIT TO BE OFFERED A SEAT AT THE TABLE.

HELP YOURSELF TO WHAT YOU WANT.

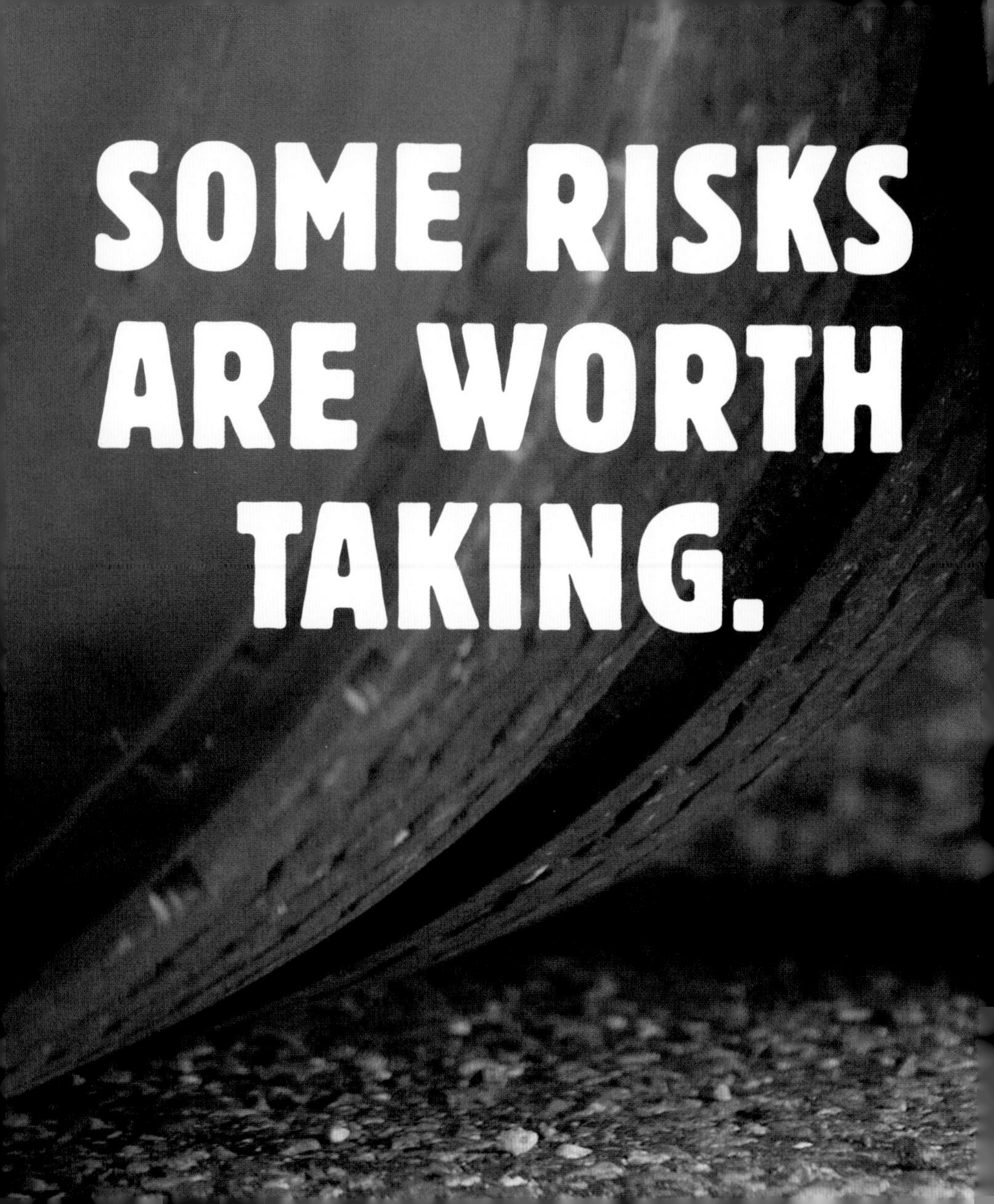
SOME RISKS
ARE WORTH
TAKING.

STICK YOUR NECK OUT.

BREAK BIG GOALS DOWN INTO SMALLER ONES.

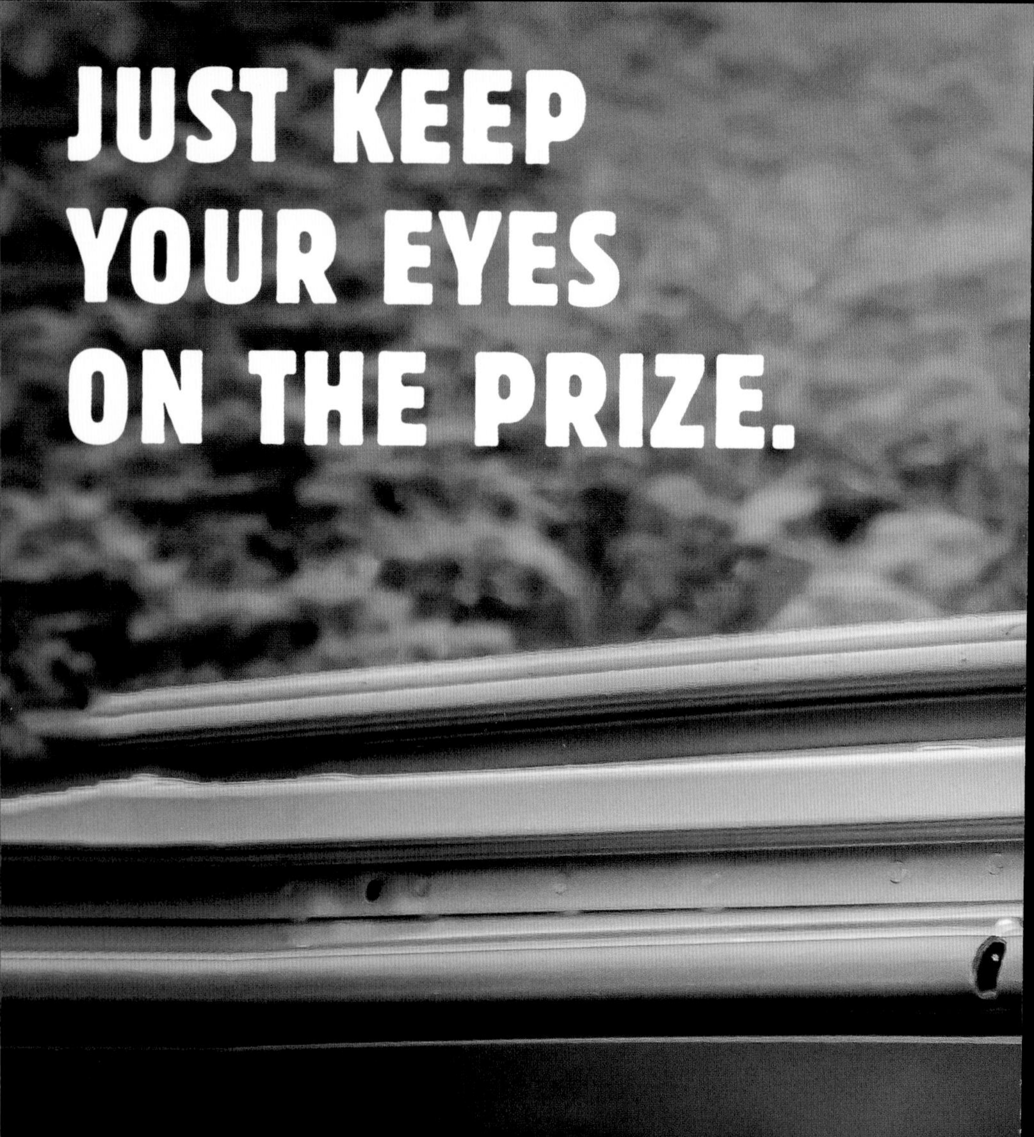
JUST KEEP
YOUR EYES
ON THE PRIZE.

COMMIT! DON'T SIT ON THE FENCE.

IT'S NOT ENOUGH TO FLY HIGH. YOU HAVE TO STICK THE LANDING.

BE BOLD.

IT'S OKAY TO RUFFLE A FEW FEATHERS.

SQUAWK LOUDLY WHEN IT'S CALLED FOR ...

BUT KNOW WHEN TO KEEP YOUR BEAK SHUT.

LISTENING CAN BE MORE POWERFUL THAN SPEAKING.

AND SILENCE SAYS MORE THAN WORDS EVER COULD.

TAKE SETBACKS IN YOUR STRIDE.

SOMETIMES ALL YOU NEED IS A FRESH PERSPECTIVE.

TRY LOOKING AT THINGS FROM A DIFFERENT ANGLE.

DON'T LET THE BAD DAYS DEFINE YOU.

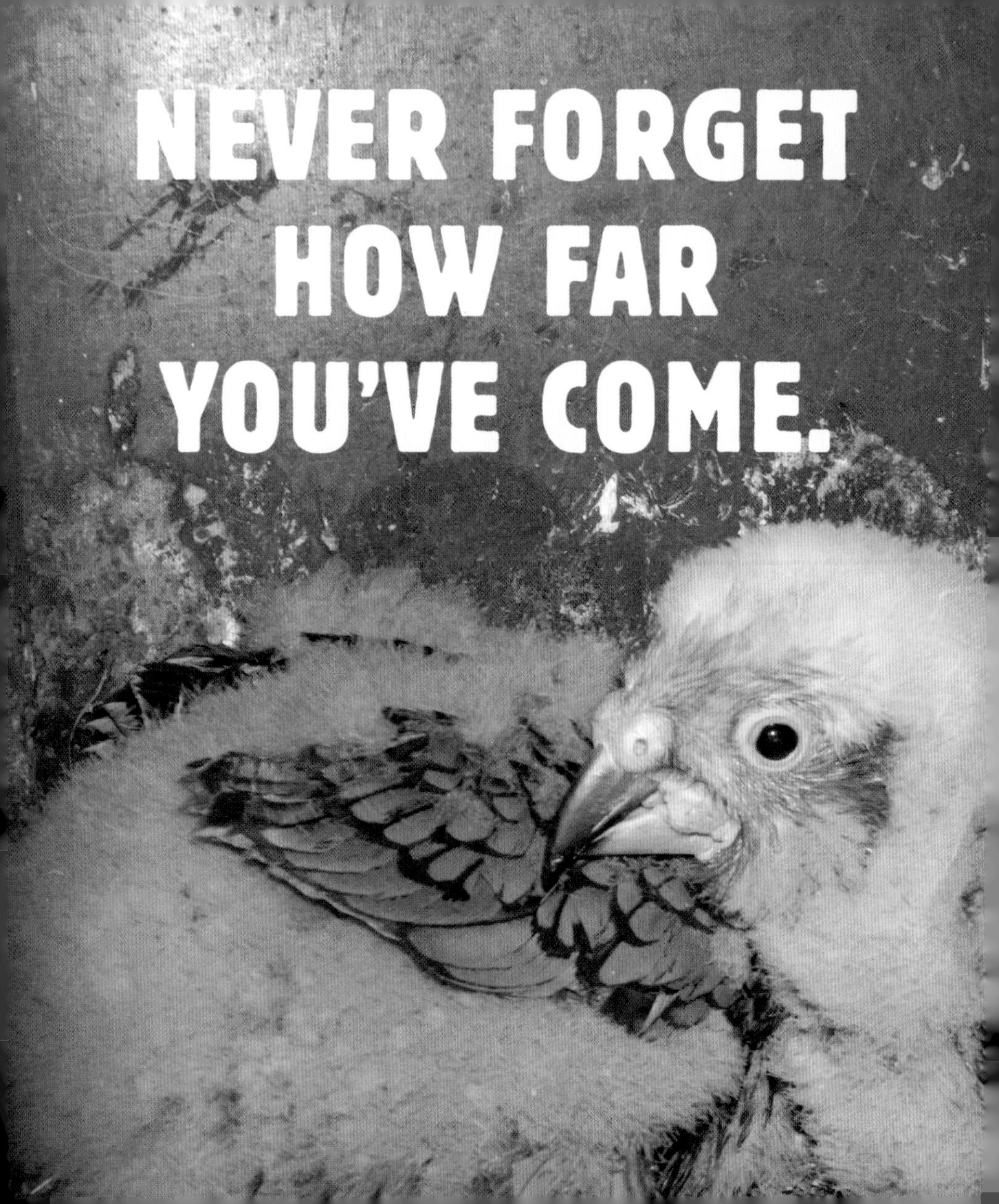
NEVER FORGET
HOW FAR
YOU'VE COME.

TAKE TIME OUT FOR PLAY ...

AND FOR SELF-CARE.

APPEARANCES MATTER.

YOU'RE MORE CONFIDENT WHEN YOU LOOK YOUR BEST.

YOUR FRIENDS
WILL KEEP YOU
GROUNDED ...

TILL YOU'RE READY TO FLY AGAIN.

YOUR DIFFERENCES ARE WHAT MAKE YOU UNIQUE.

BE A DOER, NOT A SPECTATOR.

A LEADER.

SOMEONE OTHERS
LOOK UP TO.

BUT DON'T BE SEDUCED BY FAME.

ONE PERSON'S TRASH IS ANOTHER'S TREASURE.

WHEN YOU'VE GOT WHAT YOU WANT, DON'T LET GO.

WORK TOWARDS
SHARED GOALS.

NOTHING IS IMPOSSIBLE ...

WHEN YOU HAVE THE RIGHT TEAM.

IT CAN BE LONELY
AT THE TOP ...

BUT THE VIEW IS AMAZING.

SPREAD YOUR WINGS. IT'S TIME TO SOAR.

DID YOU KNOW?

Kea are endemic to Aotearoa New Zealand. Māori gave them their name, describing the sound they make: *kee-aa*.

Waitaha Māori viewed kea as the guardians of the mountains. They are the world's only alpine parrots.

Less than 40 per cent of kea survive their first year. But those who do can live 20 years or more in the wild.

You can spot juvenile kea by the yellow ring around their eyes.

With their grey-green plumage, kea are all business on top, but they're party underneath, with black and yellow bands beneath their brilliant blue wings, and dazzling orange 'armpit' feathers that glow under UV light.

The kea's species is *Nestor notabilis*: Nestor was a wise old warrior in ancient Greece, and *notabilis* means 'noteworthy' in Latin. A suitable name for the world's wisest bird!

Kiwis love their kea! The kea was named the country's bird of the year in 2017 and took out third place in a recent national poll to find the 'Bird of the Century'.

Harper *by* Design

An imprint of HarperCollins*Publishers*

HarperCollins*Publishers*
Australia • Brazil • Canada • France • Germany
Holland • India • Italy • Japan • Mexico • New
Zealand • Poland • Spain • Sweden • Switzerland
United Kingdom • United States of America

First published in 2024
by HarperCollins*Publishers* (New Zealand) Limited
Unit D1, 63 Apollo Drive, Rosedale, Auckland 0632,
New Zealand
harpercollins.co.nz

A catalogue record for this book is available from
the National Library of New Zealand

ISBN 978 1 7755 4269 8 (hardback)

Publisher: Mark Campbell
Publishing director: Brigitta Doyle
Project editor: Elizabeth Cowell
Copywriter: Jess Cox
Cover and internal design by Mietta Yans,
HarperCollins Design Studio

Front cover image: Lost in Time/Shutterstock
Back cover images: Tom Kolossa/iStock, Sebastien
Goldberg/Unsplash
Endpapers: Joshua Fawcett/Shutterstock
Photography: *Alamy Stock Photo:* p. 28, Carsten Lampe;
pp. 46–47, Radoslav Cajkovic; p. 73, Jaap Bleijenberg;
pp. 100–101, 109, Andrew Walmsley; pp. 102–103,
patla/Stockimo; p. 108, Andy Trowbridge/Nature
Picture Library, Galaxiid; p. 110, ART Collection, Zoonar
GmbH/D-72555 Metzingen; p. 111, Mark Carwardine/
Nature Picture Library, Natalia Paklina/Buiten-Beeld |
Getty Images: p. 4, Andrea Janas; pp. 34–35, James Yu;
p. 62, Daniel Garrido; pp. 68–69, Stephane Godin;
pp. 90–91, Helmut truecolors/500px | *iStock:*
pp. 14–15, 65, Jack Burden; pp. 32–33, oneclearvision;
pp. 40–41, Tom Kolossa; pp. 42–43, aimintang;
p. 48, NanoStockk; p. 57, nztrevor; pp. 70–71, Imogen
Wamgert; pp. 92–93, Kamadie; p. 94, PK6289;
pp. 96–97, Sean Cooper | *Nature Picture Library:*
p. 99, Andrew Walmsley | *Shutterstock:* pp. 3, 106,
Lost in Time; p. 6, Petter Svensson; pp. 8–9, Gabor
Kovacs; p. 10, Lei Zhu; p. 19, Uwe Aranas; pp. 20, 88,
Sheryl Watson; pp. 22–23, Lln4plc; pp. 26–27, Angela
Meier; p. 31, Kanokrat Thaiwatcharamas; p. 38, Frank
Fichtmueller; pp. 45, Rowan Annie; p. 52, Sthapana
Sriyingyong; p. 54, Stanislav Fosenbauer; p. 58, Imogen
Warren; pp. 66–67, belizar; p. 77, Shaun Jeffers; p. 78,
ChameleonsEye; pp. 84–85, Viktor Hejna; pp. 86–87,
udeyismail; pp. 104–105, Jumussoi94 | *Unsplash:*
p. 13, Tobias Stonjeck; pp. 16–17, 36–37, 83, Sebastien
Goldberg; p. 25, Maksim Shutov; pp. 51, 60–61, Karl
Anderson; p. 74, Matthias Speicher; p. 80, Andreas Sjovall
Colour reproduction by Splitting Image Colour Studio,
Wantirna, Victoria
Printed and bound in China by RR Donnelley

8 7 6 5 4 3 2 1   24 25 26 27 28